Chaosmos

Donated by
Tavern Books
Portland, OR

© DEMCO, INC.— Archive Safe

Chaosmos

Magda Cârneci

Translated by
Adam J. Sorkin & Magda Cârneci

TERRA INCOGNITA SERIES: VOLUME 9

WHITE PINE PRESS / BUFFALO, NEW YORK

Publication of this book was made possible, in part, by with public funds from the New York State Council on the Arts, a State agency.

Cover collage by Magda Cârneci, copyright ©2004 by Magda Cârneci and used by permission of Editura Paralela 45, Piteşti & Bucureşti, Romania.

Acknowledgments:
    Adam J. Sorkin and Magda Cârneci express thanks to Călin Vlasie, President, Editura Paralela 45, for permission to use Magda Cârneci's cover collage and for the English rights to the poems in *Haosmos şi alte poeme* (2004).
    Adam J. Sorkin gratefully acknowledges the support of the National Endowment for the Arts in the form of a Translation Grant in Poetry to complete this book.
    Appreciation is also offered to the editors and publishers of the following periodicals and anthologies, in which versions of the translations in this book have appeared: *Apostrof, Calende, Cimarron Review, Exquisite Corpse, The Greensboro Review, International Feminist Journal of Politics, Krasnogruda, Orient Express, The Poetry Miscellany, Respiro, Romanian Civilization, The Southern California Anthology, The West Wind Review; Romania and Western Civilization/România şi civilizaţia occidentală*, ed. Kurt W. Treptow, *Day After Night: Twenty Romanian Poets for the Twenty-First Century*, ed. Gabriel Stănescu and Adam J. Sorkin, *Romanian Poets of the '80s and '90s: A Concise Anthology*, ed. Andrei Bodiu, Romulus Bucur, Georgeta Moarcăs, *Speaking the Silence: Prose Poets of Contemporary Romania*, ed. and tr. Adam J. Sorkin with Bogdan Ştefănescu.

First Edition

10-digit ISBN: 1-893996-78-6
13-digit ISBN: 978-1-893996-78-6

Printed in the United States of America

Library of Congress Control Number: 2006923280

White Pine Press / P.O. Box 236 / Buffalo, New York 14201
www.whitepine.org

Chaosmos

Chaosmos

Introduction by Richard Jackson:
Inhaling the World's Body: The Poetry of Magda Cârneci / 11

Foreword by Adam J. Sorkin:
The Harmonization of Contraries and the Counterpoint of Translation / 18

I. The Vision

Flashgun. Photograph. Slow Developing / 29
Siamese Sister / 31
Into the Body / 34
A Sea of Flames / 35
In the Last Light / 37
Cosmic Magnolia / 39
Blue Iris of Infinity / 40
Red. Purple. Blood / 42
Portrait of a Flash / 44
In Brâncovean Style / 46
Huge Wing / 48

II. Cosmic Burial

Cosmic Burial 1-9 / 53

III. And the World

Loved Nevertheless / 67
Night Garden / 69
The Green Kiosk in the Public Gardens / 72
Hyacintha / 73
Dark Orchid / 74
Couple Poem / 76
An Amphitheater in Greece / 78
Ana Ipătescu of the Block / 79
Psalm / 82
By Hope / 84
Chaosmos / 86

IV. Post-Manifesto

A Vast Reader / 89

Notes on the Poems/ 91

The Author/ 93

The Translator / 93

"That I no longer reveal, that I no longer interpret,
but that I transform consciousness itself into a drug
and through it attain vision and the world."

—Roland Barthes

Inhaling the World's Body:
The Poetry of Magda Cârneci

Richard Jackson

In his little essay, "The Mythologizing of Reality," Bruno Schulz wrote that while the development of language consists in stretching the meanings of words until language is "torn apart" into everyday speech, "forms adapted to practical needs," until language itself "loses its grip" and is subjected to new rules that society and government dictate, the job of the poet is to discover where "short circuits of sense occur between words, a sudden regeneration of the primeval myths." This, he says, is poetry. As part of the poetic experience, he adds, one enters a kind of dream world, a world that seems beyond us but also confronts us every day, a world that is as mist-filled as it is solid. In Magda Cârneci's terms, it is a world that is chaotic on the local level and cosmically ordered on a larger scale—a chaosmos, something akin to what modern physicists call chaos theory.

In this context one can see why her lines move so eclectically and associatively, but always aim ultimately at an intense, almost Blakean vision, and why there is a counterpointing between a kind of swirling cloud of abstractions that suggest an unknowable cosmos and the very concrete, everyday details through which the self starts to experience the cosmos. "In the end / disorder reaches perfection," she writes in the title poem, a perfection imaged in a "daring and profound photograph," an image that threads its way through many of these poems. And yet that end is not an end, for a Saturn-like creature grasps the photo "and gulps it down" after dialectically examining it and himself "for a long, long time." Temporality enters again at the end of the poem. The movement suggests not finality but a perfection that is a dialectic movement itself.

For example, in "Into the Body," the third poem of the book, Cârneci begins by focusing on everyday details and then suddenly moves to "the frantic / proliferation of cosmic and microbial realms":

I would like to inhale the entire world into the body:
    acid sunsets, electric cities and snow,
        the dead in the field, soaring dawns and the clatter and honk
    of the streets in the morning, relentless migrations and the frantic
        proliferation of cosmic and microbial realms.
That the entire world would swarm into me
    through my skin, my nails, my blood
        to saturate me   overwhelm, destroy, dissolve me.

This desire to be absorbed into the larger, nearly chaotic, cosmos, to be "dissolved," constitutes one of the defining impulses of Cârneci's vision. But only one. For the lines go on:

That I would abide like a pebble under its enormous,
    heavy cascade, annihilated and happy:
        that I would be a mere point
                    over which a mighty ocean looms   suspended.

What seemed at first to be a dissolving into the cosmos becomes in these lines a demarcation of boundaries: the self is a point and the cosmos, distinct, is suspended over the self. Further, our perspectives also undergo redefinition, for when she looks she sees the bottom of the oceanic cosmos, and then goes on to re-describe the process of absorption:

And suddenly the ocean would burst, like a distended plastic bag
    of salt water, a gigantic placenta,
it would wash over me   wave upon wave

              flood upon flood,
but this tide wouldn't kill me: instead,   enveloping me in an instant,
     it would scour my blood   course through my veins and arteries
like an enormous roar   with a blinding brilliance like lightning
                              threading through a needle's sharp point.

This is no mere repetition, of course, for the terms have changed: it is not an end but a beginning, a rebirth, and the cosmos would not dissolve her but rather enter her. The individual and the cosmos become one, as the cosmos, now personified, would

       assume a body   and be born,
          not to disintegrate me   not at all to die.
Nothing less than the entirety of the world   would fulfill me.
     That I would absorb it into the body. That I would be world.

What is crucial here is not the final result but the process, the dialectic process that occurs again and again in various forms under various themes: the poems, and the entire book, move by this symphonic process of suggesting, qualifying and further suggesting. It is an endless process, for Cârneci understands the essential role of poetry as not to provide simplistic answers but to provide process, a way of thinking that points towards possible solutions.

That is why there is so much of the subjunctive and conditional in these poems, whether given overtly or in visionary suggestions, as in "Blue Iris of Infinity" which is characterized by use of the conditional "might." And yet, as in that poem, the conditional becomes so insistent that the desire becomes a present, even in some cases a past. "I am with you," she repeats in that poem, as she moves towards "a huge Yes" that surmounts the qualifications and worries about her possible relationship that is the poem's ultimate subject.

The conditional expresses a desire, a will—so many of these poems are love poems, but a transcendent as well as physical love. And the dialectic between the enormous and overpowering will of the world, the cosmos, and the imaginative will of the individual traces itself back to Schopenhauer's sense of a double knowledge gained from the interaction of these two perspectives. For Schopenhauer, as for Cârneci, the world is always abstract when seen in its cosmic dimensions, and it is the job of the poet to give it substance through the continuing process of making poems. In *The World as Will and Representation*, Schopenhauer writes: "the abstract concepts that are the direct material of poetry . . . must be so arranged that their spheres intersect one another, so that none can continue in its abstract universality, but instead of it a perceptive representative appears before the imagination, and this is then modified further and further by the words of the poet."

Poetry is, as Paz says, "metamorphosis, change, an alchemical operation."

We see this in the very first poem where the poet and a "we" (a lover, all of us) are "stretched out on beds" on which someone has tossed photos of them, "heaps of photos," where the individuals become *representations* of themselves, part of the *"great happening"* as the repeated phrase keeps insisting, a world of "images upon images," a world that is itself "a *boundless image.*" The dialectic between the individuals, their images and this larger "happening" gradually metamorphoses towards a recognition that the world is represented in "a photo /   of another   much bigger photo." Indeed, the characters become photos themselves, undeveloped, waiting at the end for someone "to develop us   to fix us in poses   and expose us." What this will lead to, finally, is a vision that will either "save the earth" or else "make it vanish." The poem acts as an interrogative prologue to which the rest of the book continually seeks to discover answers: does our vision of the cosmos dehumanize us or define us as individuals, or both, is the essential question here.

A number of Cârneci's poems examine this issue by focusing on individuals, as does the poem, "In the Last Light," which opens with her observing a poor woman by the side of the road claiming a small space of her own by spreading out her few feeble objects. That the poet sees through the imperfect dirty window of a bus not only suggests the limitations of anyone's vision and understanding but also allows her to remember other people and other places before returning to the woman to offer recognition in the form of alms. Upon seeing her, she quickly realizes the woman has her own world, made material by the objects she has accumulated, but she also signifies a much greater, immaterial role, an archetypal female principle, both holy virgin and "wet nurse." What happens next is the sort of vision that Cârneci regularly salvages from such scenes: she sees the woman "in the pit of the universe, / lonesomely gazing at the smoking world, the wasteland." Suddenly the perspectives are reversed: the woman becomes not an observed being but the center of a bleak world that includes the narrator, a world beyond them both and "resolving into itself."

We can see this dialectic sort of reversal in her long, nine-part poem, "Cosmic Burial," which begins with a sense of how "gravity forsakes me" as the cosmos seems to expand through the next several sections into a vast, "blind" chaotic space that is all "Frantic ascension   illimitable." Still, it is also something that can be known or sensed by individuals, by language:

I, a voice I give you   to describe this universe unraveled
into the chasm of your thought   a tongue I give you to taste
its nonbeing

Later, at the center of this chaos, she discovers "the face of a little girl / a blond Alice," and realizes that "this universe is feminine" and therefore at least potentially life giving. Perhaps, then, the chaos is only what we make of it, our Schopenhauerian representation? She seems to suggest this in part 9 where she begins by countering the opening of the sequence with the phrase "gravity finds me again" and goes on to say:

I am sitting on the sea wall   at a table buried in drifted sand
    and munching on words   dead dried mollusks   a universe of
dried words   destroyed   by their proximity to the void
    to its cold absolute
all around a red, sonorous sea   words words words   slowly rising
    over the sand   over the ankles
there are dead fish in the water   archaic shells   rusty coins

These things, as the American poet Wallace Stevens says in "The Man on the Dump," are what imagination uses to create a new world, a new vision. "What is the I?" the waves of things surrounding Cârneci ask, and she replies with a vision spoken by a little child, a new birth from her feminine universe: "every-thing   everything."

Having arrived at and defined the center of chaos, she can move, in the third section of the book, to more personal poems since the self, through the processes of the first half of the book, now also holds the world inside it. "I myself was the whole world" she says in "Loved Nevertheless," the opening poem of the third section. It is in this section that she wishes to redeem the world, "to intone a new vegetal euphony of goodness / retrieve for you the flowers' ancient green language" in which she herself once blossomed. Now the hugeness of the cosmos is reflected in the complexity of everyday life, the "labyrinthine pathways" of "Night Garden." However, this is not a simple materialistic world, for Cârneci constantly sees beyond the objects themselves, sees their shimmer, their "energies   frequencies," as the image of the swirling cosmos of the first section gives way to a variety of garden images, the cosmic flowers to the real flowers in this section, even people seen as flowers ("Hyacintha"). The lover becomes the "Dark Orchid" who inspires both fear and attraction such that she asks, "Is it only through death I can touch your love?" So many of the poems of this third section focus on the thingness of things while not losing track of their potentially transcendental shimmer: a Greek amphitheater, an historical figure, minerals, flowers, the addressee.

Strangely a note of guilt enters this third section, perhaps born of the sense of lost love that so permeates the poems. The cosmic absences of the first section have become the personal losses the poet feels, losses that are themselves, like the guilt of their loss, "boundless, unpardonable." At the end of the section she turns to hope and to prayer, to "something like divine, cosmic love. // Or maybe, long ago, I have already fallen here to my knees?" Here she can project the past and remember the future, for the physical world she finds herself rooted in is also defined by a "flickering between chiaroscuro and light," a visionary stance that, as the title of this poem insists, is defined "By Hope." The poem ends on a prophetic note that is also a geologic history: "For diamond is awakened coal." So, too, we are meant to think, is the self, holding the history of its carbon, its past, as it looks forward to a future that is "radiant."

Cârneci's last poem of the book, a kind of epilogue, projects us as her "Vast Reader," each of us a self that contains a world, that involves itself in her dialectic of object and cosmos, particular and universal, the real and the imagined:

> he will encompass in the boundless blue crystal of his eye, and also
> the single strand of hair that the abandoned woman, in her piety,
> picks with tweezers from the scarf her lover left behind, the hyper-
> bolic mind of the species, the sophisticated chess of civilizations,
> the poetical systems of nature, Morel's invention, desperate utopias
> and fairy-tale nightmares—every one of these things he will

encompass in the dazzling crystalline lens of his single, all-embracing eye—and the mustard seed, too, the dot on the letter *i* and this planet

Like Stevens's ideal reader, he is part text, part of the vision that he sees, so that his relationship to the world, to these poems, is a kind of metaphor for how we deal with our worlds:

> . . . only metaphor still can bear the crushing weight of past time, its endless gaze far behind, its endless gaze far ahead, when only poetry will go on pulsing through its veins the blood of resurrection.

The Harmonization of Contraries and the Counterpoint of Translation

Adam J. Sorkin

It has been a privilege to work with Magda Cârneci on the English trans-lation of the poems in her book entitled *Chaosmos*—a neologism that has a pedigree but may at first glance elicit puzzlement. It's many things: a paradox, a dialectic, a portmanteau word packing together *chaos* and *cosmos,* and a pun derived from James Joyce's *Finnegans Wake* by way of Umberto Eco (later also adopted by the French philosophers Gilles Deleuze and Félix Guattari). To Cârneci, it's all these and more. In a recent e-mail to me she explained, "I found the term so appropriate to my own sense of oxymoron as a main tool in poetry and to my search for '*coincidentia oppositorum,*' or 'harmonization of contraries,' which is a constant obsession of my inner quest, so to speak, that I immediately made this term mine in a deep way."

The poet Magda Cârneci is a major figure in the strong and vital Romanian poetic tradition as well as a world voice whose creative roots have also been nurtured in Europe, particularly France, and in America, to which, before the fall of the totalitarian communist state in late December, 1989, she could travel only through her reading. Cârneci has been lauded as the outstanding poet of the 1980s generation which reinvented Romanian poetical practice and ambi-tions. The "eighties-ists," to translate literally the label often used in Romanian, were a very talented and daring group of younger writers. Marginalized, on the outskirts of the literary landscape and society in gener-al, they felt themselves disaffected from the richly elaborated traditions of modernist writing that had successfully and very fruitfully dominated their native poetry since the enforced hegemony of socialist-realism ended in the late 1950s. Equally important, however, is the fact that the '80s generation felt just as thoroughly estranged from the repressive, deprived, centralized world around them, with its hypocritical ideological principles based on a single, clearly failed social, political and cultural model. Not all '80s writers were openly dissidents, as Cârneci became, but all were heretics at heart.

Cârneci began her career as a prominent member of this "blue-jeans gener-ation," a nickname bestowed in recognition of a countercultural style that owed something to the American Beats and the hippies of the '60s. The "eighties-ist" writers themselves self-consciously advanced the cause of their generation under the flag of postmodernism. This term suggests much more than the stylistic rebellion and sometimes effete experimentalism the notion could give rise to in the West. In southeastern and central Europe, postmod-ernist concepts were no luxury effect of highly developed post-industrial con-sumer societies, to say the obvious. Indeed, the democratic, pluralistic tenden-cies of postmodernist thought inherent in its questioning of institutions and ideologies can be understood as an essential dimension of its appeal as beto-kening a potential new relationship to both state and artistic production behind the Iron Curtain. From the start, Cârneci was one of the leading the-orists of postmodernism and a most articulate poetic exemplar of how art responds to what, even before the 1989 revolution, was accepted as a funda-mental paradigm shift in understanding and representing (or, rather, project-ing) the world in its polymorphous relationships to the equally protean indi-vidual human psyche.

Thus the postmodern moment in Romania that Cârneci helped to define became the opening to a wide variety of poetic experiment and high ambition, both before and after the fall of the party-state. But compared to the relative-ly thinly textured, anything-goes innovation-for-innovation's-sake of many later post-communist writers, Cârneci's characteristic poetic practice serves to transform the ordinary, the personal and biographical, the arbitrary and accidental, into a vision of beauty. *Chaosmos* renders a de-centered, deconstructed world of detailed observation and powerful feeling, an ironic world of alienation, isolated syntagms, an instant's perceptions (as if in the flash of a photograph, to use an image set forth in the opening poem). But at the same time, in a singular way, the poems heighten this world of random, unadorned factuality in a metaphysical direction, suggest the mystical immanence of order, hint that this order signifies a oneness with an orderly cosmos, imply a beyond, a design if not a designer. Cârneci has described postmodernism as an "atmosphere of doubt, insecurity and uncertainty, a vast questioning." This pervasive interrogation of everything is perhaps the other side of the imaginative coin to the "the vast wing" of seeing and being in the poem, "Huge Wing," or the "Vast Reader" of the prose poem that closes the book, "pulsing through its veins the blood of resurrection." It is not surprising that she views postmodernism as having been domesticated in Romania (as elsewhere) as a dichotomy: on the one hand, a rejection of, and opposition to, the period known as the modern, but, on the other, an opportunity for the completion of modernist cultural endeavors, a kind of traditionalism. In her work, questioning and doubt reach a "perfection," as Richard Jackson's introduction observes—a "splendor," two negations making more than a positive, as it were.

Magda Cârneci was born in 1955 in the village of Gârleni near the city of Băcau in the northeast of Romania, educated locally and in Bucharest, where she graduated in 1979 from the Institute of Fine Arts "Nicolae Grigorescu" with a specialization in art history and theory. Almost two decades later, in 1997, she earned a doctorate in art history from the École de Hautes Études en Sciences Sociales in Paris. Meanwhile, she had made her debut in print as a poet under the pen name of Magdalena Ghica, publishing two books which were enthusiastically and perceptively received by Romanian critics: *Hypermateria* (1980) and *A Deafening Silence* (1985). The eminent man of letters Nicolae Manolescu (whose "Monday Literary Circle" nurtured the gifts of many of the '80s poets in the underground literary life of the era, including Cârneci) hailed *Hypermateria* as "full of talent and originality, impressive in its realism, . . . language and imagination, in its discursive capacity, something rarely used with facility, and in the clarity of its program." Manolescu calls her "the poet . . . best able to express the lyric aspirations of poets of the new generation. . . ." At the end of the same decade, critic and scholar Eugen Simion, current President of the Romanian Academy, similarly characterized *Hypermateria* as "emblematic of most of the poetry of the 'eighties generation': a new pact with reality, an integrative poetry, aspiring to comprehend the totality of the world. . . ."

A Deafening Silence was greeted as an extension of the at once passionate and thoughtful poetry of her first book, a further development but also a bold departure. Ion Bogdan Lefter, a fellow member of the decade's literary scene, wrote in review, "Her first volume . . . risked all and won by proposing a lucid form of programmatic poetry, problematizing reality and making visible—in its way—the theoretical link between the 'quotidianist' direction and the 'abstractist' direction of cutting edge poetry. In her second volume, Magda Cârneci leaves behind that middle course and engages equally courageously on a visionary path. . . ."

Soon after I first met Cârneci in Bucharest in the summer of 1991, we began a poet-translator (and co-translator) relationship, working on a few of the poems from *A Deafening Silence.* Her two books were out of print—she had to give me photocopies; I still have them, separate, neatly sewn gatherings with hand corrections and deletions on the pages. We also collaborated on English versions of new poems of hers, part of a political phase when Cârneci, after having been involved in protests against the Ceaușescu dictatorship, also lent her services to the subsequent provisional government and then proceeded to help establish the Group for Social Dialogue, an alliance of independent intellectuals and artists supporting the values of a free, democratic post-communist society. I found myself moved and fascinated by her work. With repeated meetings and a correspondence facilitated by e-mail as we undertook our translation of *Chaosmos* about a year after it was put into print in the autumn of 1992, our acquaintance has grown into a friendship.

Cârneci's *Chaosmos* (*Haosmos* in Romanian), comprised of poems written between 1985 and 1989, represents a kind of culmination of the poetic tendencies described by commentators on her two prior books. This unified collection became the first book of hers to come out under her own name. She had originally adopted a pseudonym because her father, Radu Cârneci, was also a poet, but after the Revolution of 1989, she reunited her poetical persona with the public self who was known to be active in the political and social ferment of the times, abandoning her artistic alter ego. This shift, she has written me in a note, "cost me a lot . . . as if I had killed a person . . . a better one than the real one"—possibly a parallel in the author's life foreshadowed by the confusion and suffering that are essential to the radiance of her achievement in the book.

Chaosmos was praised as a major work as soon as it was published. Critic and prose writer Ovid S. Crohmâlniceanu noted, "Magda Cârneci . . . is not merely another voice among many others of the 'eighties generation,' but a very distinct one, one of an authentic and very gifted poet. I feel compelled to talk about her with passion. There are ethereal poets and volcanic poets: Magda Cârneci belongs to the latter." Curiously, fellow poet Traian T. Coşovei likewise resorted to a high-temperature geological figure of speech to commend her work: "The alluvial stream of reality flows like a torrent of lava in a poetic text of remarkable suggestiveness. . . . There is in this book an obsession with the vital principle, a search within the labyrinth for the mechanisms that create and keep life going. . . . The poetry of Magda Cârneci soars in this polarity: the terrifying immateriality of vision and the 'shrill' concreteness of the physical world. This volume, *Chaosmos,* gives the overwhelming sensation of a 'vast' . . . consciousness capable of perceiving everything simultaneously."

I think it natural for a critic to reach for such grand terms about *Chaosmos* because the book itself reaches so far, and does so with a power that crosses languages and cultures. There are moments when I hear Whitmanesque overtones of psychic liberation—though Cârneci corrected this impression when I mentioned it by adding that mystical Orthodox elements also play a role. Yet what to me is most impressive about the volume is the composure the poetic voice achieves by the end of the sequence of poems, her deeply felt acceptance of life, love and loss, being and nonbeing, materiality and immateriality, the individuality of the self, and both abstract and personal death. The book evinces more than intimations of immortality, survival in art as necessarily conspiring with a spiritual dimension. Implicit in many of the poems is the poet as a mature woman, not just the symbolic "little girl / a blond Alice" by some quirk fallen out of Lewis Carroll to "the center of the galaxy" in "Cosmic Burial" but the adult Magda at the center and the horizons of her created verbal universe. It should not be surprising that this universe is feminine in its imaginative space-time coordinates. *Chaosmos* is an assured, richly significant book, a profound personal synthesis.

Chaosmos was reprinted in Romania after a dozen years as part of Cârneci's collected poems, *Chaosmos and Other Poems.* It is the slightly rearranged order of this 2004 printing that we follow here. We have included in our English version all of the poems from the original volume, minus two in the first section that the poet chose to omit.

Between these editions of *Chaosmos*, Cârneci had published *Political Poems* (2000), a dual-language book simply titled *Poeme/Poems* (1999, containing earlier versions of some of these translations and additional poems in collaborative versions with me), other collections translated into French and German, and a compilation of occasional prose and interviews, *Poetrix* (2002). Two books of critical and theoretical essays also appeared, *Art of the '80s: Texts About Postmodernism* (1996, mostly in Romanian) and *Art of the 1980s in Eastern Europe: Texts on Postmodernism* (1999, in English). *The Visual Arts in Romania: 1945-1989*, derived from her doctoral treatise, came out as a book in Romanian in 2000. Cârneci also curated important art exhibitions in Romania as well as in London and Thessaloníki, where she organized the inaugural Balkan Biennial. She continues to write essays in Romanian and French as well as pursue her manifold activities. She has received grants from the Fulbright Foundation, Getty Trust, Soros Foundation, European Union, French government and, recently, Cité Internationale des Arts in Paris. After serving as a visiting professor of modern Romanian literature at INALCO (L'Institut national des langues et civilisations orientales) in Paris from 2001 to 2005, Cârneci, in 2006, became deputy director of the Romanian Cultural Institute in the city where she has lived off and on for the past decade, regularly shuttling back to Romania. Currently she is working on a new book of poetry, *Fem*, a further expression of the full identity of her poetic self as a woman, or perhaps it's better to say, of her human identity and the depth of her spirit as a woman in art.

A translator of poetry has to be like a chimera, a trans-species beast with the obsessed heart of a loyal fan of the writer he is concentrating on, and, to work best, the sober head of a ruthlessly detached practitioner of his craft. When the main translator, the expert in the target language, is a man and the poet a woman (even though she is co-translator, too), this creature may be said to be a trans-gendered beast as well. Successful translation is always a remarkably intimate process of getting to know another's self through its written traces in its original language as well as its respiration between the lines. It is a transgressive effort not just to enter another's psyche empathetically and intellectually but literally to become it, to be another's tongue and soul in the new words of the target language.

As we worked together, Cârneci would provide a first English version, most of the time with numerous changes and rearrangement of phrases, maybe deletions, maybe new images, and I would react with editing and polishing (this is not to imply her English versions weren't up to snuff; they were quite good!). In addition, I would respond with my own suggestions and further modifications. Often, having gone over the poems side by side against the Romanian originals, I challenged her English variants, not infrequently to return the poem closer to the Romanian in order to retrieve images or a pattern of lines the omission of which I perceived to be a loss. But just as frequently, Cârneci's modifications were so obviously the result of inspired second thoughts that they had to remain untouched. At moments, I hazarded a freedom of my own, especially in response to her express charge to me early in our collaboration that I should pay primary heed to the cadences and silences in English, the rhythmic heart, the throb of her poetry's development (though I believe Magda's imperative was based on trust that I would be faithful to her images and ideas). Such liberties are easiest to try out when the author herself will soon be figuratively looking over my shoulder, assenting to them or politely—once in a while more vehemently—rejecting them.

Our give and take had to be an open and direct conversation, a negotiation in the context of mutual respect and understanding, let alone consonant ideas of esthetic aim and quality, so I think it will surprise Magda when I admit now that translating her poems did not come easily to me. This was neither because of any doubts I had about their quality nor because they are forbiddingly difficult to read and enjoy on the surface. The voice and movement of images, the music of phrase and line, the play of suggestion, make for considerable immediate pleasure. To my surprise, what was hardest was the emotional impact of their lyricism, the hypnotic, incantatory effect that I discovered I kept resisting as a reader, in a kind of stubborn countermeasure reinforced by conscious effort, my need to remain, at some level, judgmental of my contribution as translator. Therefore, my initial reading and working experience was disjunctive, entropic, even anti-esthetic, as I struggled toward ways of recreating a verbal cosmos corollary to the poet's, the same ideal logos in a new linguistic medium. Yet the more I resisted and struggled, the more I was drawn in, and the more the recalcitrant self was blown away.

Somehow—and I recognize this as typical of the journey of translation, for me—I never truly saw and experienced each poem until late in the process of its transformation, usually only when reading over the nearly finished English poem. Clearly, nonetheless, the poems of *Chaosmos* had their way with me despite my arm's-length relation to them as translator. Now I have come to realize that, with what must have been a sort of negative capability, in Keats's apt phrase, my imagination seems to have channeled Magda's sensibility. In a manner of speaking, her poems managed by means of their own power to translate themselves through me, to achieve their music in counterpoint with the translator. That they did so is nothing less than testimony on my part to the way Magda Cârneci's poetry dramatizes the mysterious workings of the psyche and, in the dialogue of the poet with the self and with the reader, evokes and—to use her own term—harmonizes contraries that inhere in the human nature. Most of all, it is my personal testimony to the way her poetry engages, then more or less overwhelms the reader in search of the joy of poetic epiphany, so as to give sophisticated utterance to a primordial urge toward completion and comprehension beyond, but also embracing, the physical self.

Magda Cârneci has written, "Really original and inspiring works are not created by relating oneself to already outdated national, state, and ideological obsessions, but through the radical internalizing of the problems of individuality." I believe she has accomplished this in *Chaosmos*. I hope the reader will share my enthusiasm and admiration.

I. The Vision

Flashgun. Photograph. Slow Developing

We lay stretched out on beds, immaculate white surfaces
    on which somebody had tossed photographs   helter-skelter
snapshots of us   false, sensual photos   strewn
    carelessly on couches   on beds   on the floor
we lay where we were tossed, looking out the windows at the city
they kept taking photos of us   every second   heaps of photos   as we lay
    at rest on beds, looking out the windows and discussing
beauty   in heaps   the *great happening*   that surrounded us

they were continually photographing our drab, dirty room
    the beds, surfaces immaculate and white, the stubbed-out cigarette butts
that littered the floor   in heaps   and we were so tired   continually
        photographed
    reclining   among wet, glossy rivers   of photos

I asked them   whether everything looked beautiful to them   whether beauty
    existed everywhere   in the heaps   in this hodgepodge   of sprawled
        bodies
    and white beds   cigarette butts   the drab, dirty room
looking out the window   they laughed   and changed a used roll
    for fresh film   finer grained, more sensitive   everything could be
could have been beautiful   so beautiful   the drab, dirty room
        cigarettes
    beds   wastepaper basket   rain spouts   the *great happening*
the gutters along the streets   the remote suburbs   higgledy-piggledy
        isolated
    the scrap heaps   virtual negatives

                        that look so good in pictures

Then do all the scraps make sense?   I asked them   as they went about
    fixing us on film   lying indolently on beds   looking out
        the windows   the heaps   crying   fainting   they laughed and
        laughed

everything has expression   *expression*   they answered
    this bare, dirty room   the desolate clouds   the scrap heaps
these are pure expression   of what?   of whom?   I asked
    of expression itself   they answered   putting in a fresh roll   of
        much more
    sensitive film   the whole world is   expression   an image
    an image that's an eyeful of images   heaps
        crammed full of these and other images   images upon images
of whom? for whom?   I asked again and again   just image
    they said   a *boundless image*   an immense photograph
and their flashguns kept going off   blinding us   in black-
    and-white or in color? I asked   letting myself be photographed
continually   not daring to move at all   a photo
    they replied   focusing a new spotlight   a million-watt reflector bulb
    and in its intensity my hands turned pale   translucent   spectral

What about us? what about us?   I asked   and what about the railroad
    stations
    and planes   the rock-hard pyramids   the heaps upon heaps
of paintings, music, books   the constellations   the teeming cities?
You are   they said   undeveloped chemical emulsion
    and then they put in a fresh roll   of even more sensitive film
a photo of what?   I repeated   dissolving   a photo
    of another   much bigger photo

We lay in repose   imaged on beds   immaculate wet, white surfaces
we stay here   lying in photographs   waiting for somebody to come
    to raise us up   and plunge us   into the zinc basin   of strong cold
        acids
    to develop us   to fix us in poses   and expose us   to an even
        stronger light
a purer light   to fog us   to blind us
and destroy at last   these dark old negatives
    beauty   the *great happening*   to save the earth
                      or make it vanish.

Siamese Sister

I sat on the old green bench in the park   surrounded by the bleakness of
            winter
      brooding for the thousandth time   over myself   this empty suit of
            clothes
      and my condition as a woman   woman
among black rotted leaves   in the dank air   asking
      and asking myself   deliriously   where had
      my girl's face gone   my teenage face   and
my invincible face   perfect as a newly-minted gold coin
      in a showcase like diamond   a crown set ablaze by angels
      a celestial annunciation   snow-white   my face
brilliant   a hologram of the moon   a flash
                                    projected on the sad, cosmic subconscious,
my milk-pale face   my androgynous face   and my face of glory
      a drop of water transformed against my will
            into cascades streams rivers   gleaming in the noonday light
            above a depthless ocean   my face a necklace
strung with mountain lakes   bluish dawn surging forth
      frantic rainbows and the aurora borealis from the pole
a round pocket mirror in the young mother's blouse   wet with milk
      how you changed into a sumptuous mirror of golden
      waters   reflecting frenzied crowds   rivers
      and suns   in a dancehall where there's no one to dance:
where had they gone, how did they get lost, into what have they flowed?

I looked around myself   green bench   soggy black soil
      splotched with dirty snow   almost mud   my face
repeating and repeating to myself: woman woman woman   not under-
            standing
      not wanting to believe   woman   wondering yet again
      woman   aggregate state   woman   worn uniform
I'm still not used to. Just as in my childhood
I was amazed by the existence of little girls   blonde or dark playthings

envied
golden angelic spheres   delighted   impossible orange foam
which my alien black sphere   could never penetrate,
I was amazed by the existence of adult women   so beautiful
goddesses each clad in a chlamys of purple
who from a high mountain very far away   beckoned with magnetic signs
terrifying as tight-shut boxes   black and red
velvet and silk   soft dangerous shells

but what could they hide?

On the old green bench   trying to remember
I sat   among the park's bare trees   black and wet, amidst
unfulfilled office workers   lost handkerchiefs   chastened old ladies
with gleaming baby carriages   fire-charred remnants   green wood
smoldering   quenched by water   a lonely man or two   women women
young and ferocious   kiosks selling pastries   girls little girls
black earth   dirty snow   and the same puzzled amazement
woman   woman   woman   why shouldn't I reconcile myself
to this body   why shouldn't I dress myself with this world   orange
foam
Siamese sister   overwhelming matron   street dancer
million-petal rose   of velvet and silk   chlamys
of purple   mother   high on your distant mountain peak
enter the mysterious box   volcanic and terrible miracle

what don't I have? what do I lack?

I sat there.
A woman passed my bench
tall and young   dressed in purple and silk   a woman
much too beautiful   young and dark   and in a trance
a frenzy   like iron filings to a magnet
I was drawn after her   down alleys   between wet black trees
and withered leaves   through the vast wintry park
then along city streets.   She seemed to remind me of something
offer me something   but what?   She seemed to call out to me
promise me something   something more precious than

my infinite shame   something like me

                                             but much more perfect.
Then I could no longer see her. I lost her on the streets. I sought her
like a young lover who for the first time glimpses his true love in a crowd
and recognizes her hair and smile among the multitude
as in a mirror shattered into millions of pieces, in the world's ocean.
I sought her like a lover   although much more modestly   desperately.

Woman, woman, what are you searching for? What does the young woman,
     the dark woman remind you of?   Siamese sister, matron, street dancer,
million-petal rose   of velvet and silk   in the mysterious box,
     are you always seeking a woman?   What does she set astir in you?
Robed in purple   undulating on a high mountain,
                                             what does she promise you?

Into the Body

I would like to inhale the entire world into the body:
    acid sunsets, electric cities and snow,
        the dead in the field, soaring dawns and the clatter and honk
    of the streets in the morning, relentless migrations and the frantic
        proliferation of cosmic and microbial realms.
That the entire world would swarm into me
    through my skin, my nails, my blood
        to saturate me   overwhelm, destroy, dissolve me.
That I would abide like a pebble under its enormous,
    heavy cascade, annihilated and happy:
        that I would be a mere point
                    over which a mighty ocean looms   suspended.

And by lifting my gaze   that I would see   its translucent bottom
swirling with rapid motion   squirming and phosphorescence:
    darkness, lustrous schools of fish, the colors of the abyss.
And suddenly the ocean would burst, like a distended plastic bag
    of salt water, a gigantic placenta,
it would wash over me   wave upon wave
    flood upon flood,
but this tide wouldn't kill me: instead,   enveloping me in an instant,
    it would scour my blood   course through my veins and arteries
like an enormous roar   with a blinding brilliance like lightning
                threading through a needle's sharp point.

Somebody or something   obscure   gelatinous   boundless
wants to descend below   into the darkness   through my skin and nails
    to assume a body   and be born,
        not to disintegrate me   not at all to die.
Nothing less than the entirety of the world   would fulfill me.
    That I would absorb it into the body. That I would be world.
This is the most powerful drug   the ultimate
    which would satisfy me   and save me.
                        But not even this.

A Sea of Flames

Sometimes I see   finding myself on the streets   among crowds,
    in the absence of any drug   except the solar light,   or
in trams   narcotized by the mass of warm, moist
    bodies   or before the amber subway exits
        pouring out fields of anonymous bright faces

I see   suddenly I see   that we are flames
flickering flames twisted by wind
long glowing cones plaited with thin rays
    small flames—red, white, golden
gliding through bus stations, windows and stores,
flame upon flame   in a fiery sea, stirring, burning, quickened drops
    flowing on sidewalks, rising in elevators
staccato flickers against the evening sky

these clothes   these shoes   these uniforms of sex
and flesh   which interrupt the ocean of fire
which separate me from all of you   and from you yourself   twin sister
                world
    coagulated fire   intensity at a standstill   o world   flimsy backdrop
soaring buildings and highways and subways
    airports and movie theaters and civilizations
over the living flames that we are   covering our incandescence

one day   at one certain moment   they will crumble, dissolve,
    disappear like a cloud of vapor and dust
swept away by a single unique hand   evaporated
    like the pale molecules of a spectral hallucinogenic gas
and we'll become   I see it   I see—
    in the clammy hospital beds, in the waiting rooms
    of the railroad stations, in the doctor's offices,
there where I recognized myself ageless and illimitable in
    strange old women and young girls, in soldiers and office workers,

in the crowds oozing like an electric lava over the streets
        at noon—
we'll be one single Body   vast, pulsating   with one composite
    Face   a brilliant overflowing   rustling everywhere in space
one Heart   endlessly throbbing   one Mouth
    all-speaking   one infinite Hearing   one immeasurable Eye
staring silently at itself   we'll be one Blood
    irrigating the void with its arteries and veins
drawing a fantastical silhouette over the darkness   one simultaneous Dream
    in the unique single Brain   pouring one cresting wave
of light   unfolding from its ghostly cocoon   one Illumination
        and one shared Death

when all of us, everyone at once,   our faces upwards, flickering flames
in a sea of flames,   all laughing, roaring with laughter,   we'll drink at
            the same time
its bittersweet fathomless chloroform, sugared by
stars, planets, visions   fallen below, quietly smoldering
all absorbed in the ultimate Thought   immense, deserted, isolated
gazing with melancholy into space, into itself   an infinitesimal point
a larva, a pupa in bloom   a small and white child
tumbling through the void   like a small and white universe
ready to start over, to be born once more   and to smile

for this world ends not in a book
this world ends in Thought.

In the Last Light

She had placed herself at the shoulder of the pale yellow highway, sitting
    precisely on the curbstone
        next to the lawn littered with dried-out flowers and worn tires.
I glimpsed her through the filthy windshield, the bus had
        just about come to a stop.
A pervasive orange light slanted flickering
        over the gas station, on the traces
        of gasoline, the fumes, and black, rotten leaves.

She had spread her kerchief on the dry grass blades,
        was arranging her squalid objects one by one,
            the wind fluttered the hem of the old coat
                over her dried-out, blue-tinged legs, over her high black, laced shoes.
I glimpsed her through the filthy windshield, an orange light, and
        I hastily got off. As the driver went to the station,
            the gasoline and black, rotten leaves, I walked nearer to look at her,
She had positioned herself on the curbstone, in the rumble of the trucks,
        was fanning out her greasy gray hair, tied with ribbons
        once pink and red,
she was at home, and on the kerchief
        she was arranging an empty lipstick tube, a tram ticket
        and a small glass ball.

In the slanting orange light I remembered
        the hippies, boys and girls, those gay wretched tribes, how
            with their sex songs and unblinking stares they had given so much
                fright
to an indignant Europe and America outraged by their mystic spittle,
        their sacred squalor and oriental sloth, and then for all of them
            to arrive at the faultless life of the most fashionable bourgeois.
I thought, too, of stray dogs, sprawled without a care
        in the middle of the street, as if on a snug sofa, during torrid summer
            days,

but what kind of parents could make bourgeois out of them?
She laid her torn kerchief down by the curbstone but she was free, free,
    much freer than I. What had I gotten off to search for?

The bus horn was blaring, sunshine was falling
    orange and slanting over the gas station, and filled with
        shame and discomfort I impulsively held out a few small bills—
            to pay her for what?
She was at home, she was watching her private TV, there were
    buses and trucks, there were black, rotten leaves, the orange light
        and the wind, there were tires and rusted, empty cans
and a dead striped kitten, she was waiting for no one, for nothing,
    but everything came surging toward her in the whirl of the highway.
And though she was much older than I was, I envied her deeply,
    for she was free, much freer than I.

The bus horn kept blaring, the light fell orange and slanting
    over the gas station, but I lingered . . .
        and suddenly it came to me—
I recognized her—she was the wet nurse, Mary, the housekeeper,
    the maidservant, the definitive woman, the ancient apocalyptic woman,
        sitting right there on the curbstone, at the mouth of the precipice,
            in the pit of the universe,
lonesomely gazing at the smoking world, the wasteland,
    life like the ebbing of blood, spittle and sperm,
        slowly withdrawing, like a vision full of mud, full of cruelty,
            an infinite curtain of light and roaring noise, fluttering
softly, babbling giddily, in the colors of the rainbow,
    slowly withdrawing with a high, clear coloratura note,
        as vast as the world, in the whirl of the highway,

        and resolving into itself.

Cosmic Magnolia

The way, when you cross a dimly-lit park in spring,
the stench of a dog dead for quite some time,
    hidden, buried under fallen leaves and darkness,
can make you crazed with its horror   and after a while
you can't help breathing it in, its pungent,
    rotten nausea,   until the moment when,
    penetrating the nuclei of your cells,   this intoxicating smell
        of decay   suddenly exalts you
like some new drug   never before known,
    much more refined   than LSD or mescal,
        than any pleasure or terror,
and, finally liberated, you breathe it deeply   the sweet, killing ether,
    the black and green ozone   dank and fermenting
    like the darkness of spring,

the same way   that wretched woman
whom I now hear   hideously lamenting   behind her window
    with yellow curtains,   overwhelmed by terrible sickness,
should she pass beyond   quickly   quickly
as if she had found the sudden courage to breathe deeply   deeply
    the cold dry chloroform of the void,
after the first unbearable horror   would discover
    the rich magnolia incense of that world,
the infinite light which absorbs her.

Aromatic light,   the musk of beginnings and ends,
your atrocious sweet pulp
    which devours us and generates us,
    which disintegrates us and reabsorbs us,
you intoxicate me with all-pervading fear,
    you dissolve me with wild, all-embracing joy
inexhaustible womb   cosmic magnolia.

Oh, how long must it be   how long until that dreamt-of fragrance?

Blue Iris of Infinity

for Dana Dumitriu

Time, a motionless body laid out northern-white
    on long white strips of cotton gauze,
entrails pushed aside, white and bluish rose, archaic
    jewels, misshapen like quaint, outmoded hand grenades,
    dismantled part by part, like some ancient hellish machine,
motionless time, pinned in place, pricked, the blood falls into test tubes
    drop by drop   and the test tubes darken:

That I might be there, together with you, that I might pass beyond
    the ashen lips, the vapid smile, beyond any border.
        Through the invisible, lustrous wall of fog, downwards, on the other
            side
of the light, its brilliant, flying curtains, among
    visions and demons, sparks and lightning,
        a dark orange tunnel, a deafening silence.
You are alone, intense color-saturated films projecting
    beside, before and behind, pervading you, flooding you,
        judging you during a long, an endless, second.
You recognize yourself as a girl, a fetus, a blinding light,
    as a dark concentrated point, a cosmic explosion, a planet
        and again as woman, girl, fetus,
yes, and then over a green meadow, you see colored spheres floating
    high among sweet rainbows and a waterfall of blue light,
        blinding light looming near, nearer, nearer:

Somebody, no, no, it's a cat, it slinks across the window ledge,
    snatches a mouthful of something served on a glass platter,
the brain, sea foam instantaneously solidified,
    a vast cloud fallen into a nutshell, a piece of
soft marble, hypnotized by one singular moment, endlessly
    repeated, that very moment, right then, a film loop
continuously projected under the blood-red velvet of the eyelids,

a white eyeball blinded by lightning's unbearable flash:
    That I might see the blood stand still in rivers and streams,
in the twilight-daybreak three blood-red suns in one sun
      and my flesh falling away as golden smoke
        and the smoke fading among islets and gulfs.
    That I might see dew and frost hang in the air, condensed into pearls,
no longer yearning to descend to glossy green leaves,
    and the little dove draw its small reddish claws
      beneath its feathers, unfurl one hundred wings and
        like a jet take off steeply into the darkness.

Somebody, a woman, is scrubbing scalpels and nickel tools,
scouring blackened scissors and trays. I can see her, see you all
from above, from every which way, I am there with you, I hear them
        whispering,
arranging candles and flowers, I am with you, they go about their business
murmuring, mopping up stains.

Rivers and streams standing still, their blue mirrors soiled
    with blood, collapsing straight downwards into the dark maw
of the instant, there to get purified, where time
    is space and disintegrates into nothingness   and out of radiation
the universe springs forth, white, foamy, in luminous waterfalls,
    out of the cosmic depths of the body, out of thoughts,
a torrent of suns, millions of blinding suns exploding forth,
    golden points in the blue iris of infinity
through which world   comes streaming, streaming   a huge Yes
    poured burning into our palms   eternally given   young matter
in the vast color of peace.

Someone passes by, a shade, and accidentally bumps into
the vessel with dark blood.
The vessel falls, shatters into pieces,
But on the floor not a trace remains.

Red. Purple. Blood

Among bright pennants and traffic lights, in the delirium of street signs,
on the screaming child's handkerchief—purple, you fall in drops,
drops, eviscerated organs gleam in butcher shops, a purple rivulet streams
on the floor into the drain, pours into the sewers, traversing
subterranean galleries, veins and arteries, a purple gilding glistens
on the boy's stick candy, a violet stain announces to the girl
her submission to the laws of this world, year after year the Mediterranean
        flings
countless shells on its shores to be pounded into powders by dye-makers
renowned for rich, rare nuances since the decline of ancient Greece,
        advertisements
in store windows and billboards shower chemical purple on pedestrians' faces,
once upon a time you were the imperial purple of Byzantium, piles of
        flame-red apples
are hawked at stands in every market, glaring neon signs flicker at bar entrances
where an iron spike meticulously splits quivering pigeon breasts,
green pistils in radiant carnivorous flowers, purple slices of meat, flowering
meat you are, in hospitals baskets packed with soiled dressings are dumped
into incinerators, fiery wounds and the blush of flames, on balconies
national flags flutter, red fabric sailing leisurely through the air, levitating
high above, roses blaze iridescent in clear cellophane, offered for sale
shimmering in buckets along the streets, beneath bright pennants, near traffic
        lights,
in the delirium of noise, street signs, advertisements, billboards—oh purple,
you fall in drops, dripping down everywhere, over everything,
dripping red, crimson, purple

blood, blood, you spurt out of the artery to the floor, splash on the ground,
pristine misery, pure horror, why am I so afraid of you,
of your bleeding blinding color? that I not lose you, that I not drink you,
that we not devour you? what savage beast howls in you, what lost archaic
        ocean?
blood, blood, who is crying out to us from within you? to what do you

reclaim us?
why do you hypnotize us? why am I terrified by you?

primitive liquid, what is hidden in your serum and red corpuscles?
there are paradises, dawns, stellar dust clouds and magnetic lights,
there are purgatories and crimes, ritual murders, pearls and noble escutcheons,
tangled roots and jungles, there are sunsets, sunrises and an unimaginable
primal fire, a tidal wave of heat and darkness, rushing, spreading, coagulating,
a tide of love and death flowing and ebbing, suffusing space,
bearing within its fluid flame suns and planets, dissolving
heavy elements and light elements, water, iron, salts, fierce lightning, minerals,
lapping nourishment over peaceful countries and lazy river estuaries,
capillaries and veins—you flower into flesh and heart which tremble
in fright, and delirious, delicious red lips, murmuring

how slowly you ooze from a cut, trickle like ink to the sheet of paper
and on the table, dribble on the chair, under the door, down to the ground,
through the drains, into the sewers, along the streets, into all the world, the
                    universe,
you fall in drops, dripping red, crimson, purple

blood, where do you come from? where do you flee when forsaking us
in thin rills, in sluggish dense streams, in a myriad of red drops?
where do you return in your exodus of corpuscles, your flame, your darkness?
where do you retreat when withdrawing from us
your prolonged wave of love and of chaos?
who receives you back? and who gives you to us again?

sacred misery, sweet horror, why am I still afraid of your substance,
of your burning blinding color? that I not lose you, that I not drink you,
that we not devour you, surging fire, living water, strange shivering vibration:
where do you go from us, blood? why do you abandon us, holy purple?

Portrait of a Flash

for Adrian Giurgea

What remains of us   after this world grants us being?
    In the cage of the tram one afternoon, the leavening of a crowd
      rusting in shops and offices for an interminable day,
a day of heated tin roofs, a day of coffee, newspapers and boredom,
    a day of asphalt turned to syrup, of popcorn and charred hamburgers,
while in bodies, in the dough, the last yawns had hardly been stifled,
    sweat, sleep and the void had hardly begun to bloom,
and in bags, peppers and cabbages, the all-purpose
    detergent and all-purpose vodka had hardly begun to sleep,
oh, sour leavening, weary crowd submerged in summer heat,
    tired of the history perpetually overhauling itself, tired of
      egos restlessly self-inventing instead of heading home
      and putting themselves to bed,
oh, obscure miracle, I have waited a lifetime to catch sight of you,
    for you to show yourself here, there, wherever,   in bottles and bags,
      in trams, in crowds   to glimpse your blue flame
      flashing at me like lightning;
but you, pale and profitless, still keep yourself
        far from our minor solar system.

The infinitesimal gods, look how crowds of ants
    are carrying them, their bright little legs flailing in the air,
    to the warm bed of compost where their translucent gelatin
    will nourish the germs of tender new generations,
and their red shells will be thrown to the antiquities museums,
they will find themselves assimilated without a trace in millions
    of perfect copies   and millions of eggs and feces,
    in millions of eyes, wings, antennas,   in fur, horn, hoof,
    millions of steel flints, plows, shovels,
    houses, boulevards, bordellos,   in gold, enigma, cosmos,
a joyous cosmos, a plenty of shopping bags and bodies, in the tram one
        afternoon,

in the leavening of a crowd:
what to pray for, then? what to look for?

What remains after this world undoes us?
   Tired, I was waiting   in the abundance of the crowd   as within
an ocean of electricity, trying to make a verse, seeking a trance-like state,
a suspended animation, an orison for the soul,   until in an instant's light-
         ning flash
   I saw the ants, tiny cones and sticks, scurrying, teeming,
   luminous waves of ants, slowly withdrawing with a rustle
like fine sand, colorless, from warehouses, markets, offices,
   from streets, asphalt and concrete,   retreating out of clothes, newspapers,
         bags,
turning back to bright little legs flailing in the air,
   I saw all that is solid suddenly swirling   as down a sink drain
toward the tiny bright gods, lilliputian cones and sticks,   dancing and free,
   free sparks,   joyously transforming into one another,
   into everything, into nothing, in a blinding vortex
where I was a spark among sparks,   an ant
   among myriads and myriads of ants.

At last, you know: humble miracle, are you enough?
Like a solitary electron in the lightless vacuum chamber
ready to fly   through the bombardment of particles and the revelation
   into an instant's fission   or into a sudden visionary flash,
   into a new universe   or new darkness,   into another fiction
      far from our minor solar system.

And so you're journeying into Bucharest by tram one afternoon,
   clanking through the suburbs . . . Chitila . . . Griviţa . . . the Avenue of
         Victory,
   to the throbbing center of the metropolis,
in the leavening of a crowd, warm and moist,
their bright little legs flailing helplessly in the air.

In Brâncovean Style

At long last I've discovered the Brâncovean church
undocumented in books, its phosphorescent projection
engraved in red only on a meninx, a map,
suddenly I found myself there, it turned out to be very near,
in a circular courtyard, forgotten and filled—but how?—filled
with huge reddish boulders, boulders of old, dry meat,
suspended in the air above the newly sprouted grass, unbelievably green.

In the vast unknown church, like an aquarium of blue-green
glass, luminous and cool, among gold-leaf haloes and painted saints
who had been awaiting me for such a long time, I caught a glimpse
of a Roman statue before the gilded altar, a solitary marble Caesar
in a short tunic of mail, gesturing upwards with his arm, pointing high above,
and as I looked at him, his eyes, as round as ancient bronze coins,
began to beam blue light, like a pair of bright headlights,
two large turquoise stones,
and lifting my gaze I viewed a vault of deep violet,
a soaring cupola with two enormous eyelids that slowly open,
letting the distant, radiant sky be seen, the evening sky
pricked by white stars and minuscule yellow moons,
and a strange red sphere, like an immense corpuscle of blood,
spinning dizzily, a great, hovering, fire-red sphere
that, approaching with an eerie whistle, enters the split cupola,
absorbs me—or maybe I was already in the far reaches of space.

Inside, there are mother-of-pearl flights of stairs and vaulted ceilings,
I keep climbing and descending through niches and labyrinths,
through shelves crammed with books, videocassettes, magazines—
nobody there, only a void, untenanted brilliance.
Thousands of CDs and records are playing
all at the same time, clocks chiming, bells tolling;
on hundreds of screens far-distant galaxies are dawning
and setting, shy big-bangs and stuttering apocalypses.

I can see sportive worlds of interstellar dust condensing and dispersing,
silver lights and mycelia interweaving, circuses of floating white clouds,
then street lamps illuminating boulevards, a little girl chasing
a big red balloon like a globular corpuscle of blood, dissolving
into a man and a woman embracing among millions of identical corpuscles.

And inside, emptiness glowing, a milky, aseptic
brilliance, thousands of CDs and records resounding,
films and videos projected everywhere, books tumbling down
from shelves to marble floors, magazine pages riffling,
and the rustle of an invisible multitude with unseen wings and antennas,
summoning me upwards, bidding me in silence to ascend,
then ascend even higher,
boosting me under my arms on landings and stairs,
through niches and labyrinths, through shelves,
up to the highest room, just below the cupola, surrounded by an ocean of
            darkness,
a plastic capsule spherical like a giant eyeball, covered by a pair of closed,
            transparent eyelids,
where I discover a perfect secretary who goes on typing, typing without a
            sound.

At last she notices me and hands me a blank sheet of paper—
an application form. And she asks me: what style would you prefer?
archaic? angelic? demonic?
gothic? modern?
            or Brâncovean?

Huge Wing

I emerge from sleep   a devil's stunted blue leg
     slams the alarm clock,
          scattering larvae and cockroaches in squadrons.
Harsh daylight. Cold water. A coffee. Clothes crammed into my bag.
     Key; elevator; street. Bus; driver; glare on the window:
and you   huge wing   slowly you unfurl
     in the bitter wind of dawn   between violet and purple
          high overhead.

Gradually the train starts to move. We talk about the war.
  The soldier unwraps his breakfast. About the Middle East.
The old woman examines her ticket and complains loudly.
  About the *logos* embodied in history. The bald man snores
rattling the newspaper across his face. Between our lips
  the dough of tomorrow's humanity rises. We talk about salvation
through struggle and suffering. Transformation. Transfiguration.
  Silence. I stare at the window.
The world goes flying by, in a blur. We watch the world from the train.
  Out the window. Hurrying past. From the train. On the window. Speeding,
careering by us. And there, above the fields, far into the distance,

something else races even faster, arrives again and again before our eyes,
something repeats itself, repeats endlessly
     stations and train yards, the skirt of the woods and yellow-green fields
     dawns, sunsets, dawns again, battlefields, towns
     traffic signals, the budding of trees, the leaves falling
     war news, men and women waiting submissively
          on platforms, then more stations, train yards, troops, fields and the
               wings of birds
something repeats itself, repeats, hurtling before us in its flight
     before our eyes, desperately,
something that would make itself seen.

Something
    that would imprint on the blind retina of our eyeballs
the composite flash
      of the entire world   gigantic: the quick spark of innumerable lovers
               embracing,
    the phosphorescent brilliance of millions of tiny existences,
    our flickers sweeping into an ocean of flames, souls
    traversing countries and continents tirelessly, aimlessly,
    loving, killing, sacrificing, devouring,
and in dark and bright patches, hovering, dancing,
  as on a cosmic merry-go-round
              the pure snapshot of REALITY—

the dazzle   of a sudden illumination
              over the imaginary sea scum of our exhausted cerebrum.
That in its camera obscura   amnesiac   would be developed
    the colossal hallucinatory   photo
    of this universe   necrotic and latent.
Yet loveable.   Its huge beauty.
That at last we would *see.*

That we no longer would live propelled forward, then back,
in trains   and   wars
    or waiting on platforms and in stations   in suburbs and airports
for a golden future   the purple doomsday of this world
    talking about the Middle East   about *logos*   about history
    alone in deserted terminals   buried beneath TV news and the day's
        papers.

That we *see.* That we live for ourselves in the moment.
The Here. The Now.
    All at once. Instantaneously.
    In a flash. In no time. A long moment, eternal.
Our body of blood, of humors and imagination,
    dissolving   through *instancy*   in the emulsion of the world's image.

That we become the Image itself. The strange Photograph.
Sensitive. Painful.

    All at once. The flash.

That we *know* with our eyes   *awaken*   our body   *awaken.*
    That we *be*   at last   the vast wing   between violet and purple
        slowly unfurling   silently   making itself seen
            high overhead.

II. Cosmic Burial

Cosmic Burial

I.

One hour later, gravity forsakes me.

You were refusing the earth   the sweet maternal clay
    the moist phosphorescent cave   the dark, hidden burrow
you rejected   the ancient atavistic thirst   to descend
    slip back into fetus   uterus   point   back
        into water   fire   metals.

Torn from the shell   plunging naked   into space   into the void
    into the unbreathable ether   searing the nostrils the flesh
so as to evaporate   to break free   to contain through
    frantic dilation   like a rare gas   its hard absolute,
        rock-hard and inexpugnable.

Like an archaic urn   floating at random   weightlessly
    scattering its extinguished ashes   among identical urns
floating   among other cosmic dreams   casting in their wake
    swarms of chaotic images   upon the stellar dust

so as no longer to have anywhere to fall to   to dwell in   to return from
    but to disappear   through fission   through vaporization
on a space voyage   among comets and nebulae
    among big-bangs   and solar spectra   you sought
a masculine grave
        in dying   so as never to die.

2.

One hour later.

Torn from beside me   from the slumberous union   from
     untouched scorching bed clothes   you hurtled
upwards   like a dizzying geyser   luminous   through the darkness
     of night   upwards   vertical   far above
     tearing the cold of the currents of night
and you were not alone   warm voices surrounded you   roaring
     as you rose with supersonic speed   joyful of depth
in the spiral of the cosmic whirlpool   hissing like a lightning flash
     past the moon   her pale mournful face   clearly divided
into shadow and light   upwards   joyful   casting
     behind you   organs and earth   remembrance and fear
higher upwards   through the purifying cold of the void
     vertiginous jet   dizzying roar   and when all the other
joyful voices   kept calling you further   did you not know fear?

did you wake?   did you dream for an instant of untouched
     scorching bed clothes   of the slumberous union?   and whom did
          you ask
to set you down   back here   below?
whose loving hand?

3.

Frantic ascension   illimitable   in a darkness named
      love   a blood of images   a celestial jet of
images   a spectral lava   where in artesian wells   in waterfalls
      young populations   delicate   astral dust clouds   nerve cells
histories   supernovas   childhood memories   cosmic dreams   are rising.
      Possible worlds sunk into one another   like the nacreous
translucent membranes of a sidereal egg
where all atoms   energies   void desert spaces   yearned for
      life   life the dream of the infinite   all matter desirous of
ardor   nebulae burning for love   white and red blood
      corpuscles   comets and meteors dreaming to copulate
the atemporal craved dissolution into the moment   the void craved
      birth   the darkness dreamed of death   transformed into
light   death itself kept dreaming   dreaming   dreaming of resurrection.
Silhouettes of women and men   embracing each other in long luminous
              chains
      embracing the darkness   clothing with their very bodies
the cosmic dream   where vision and extinction   are one and the same
      where out of their lightning   could arise
          the dawn of a new form of life.

4.

I, a voice I give you   to describe this universe unraveled
into the chasm of your thought   a tongue I give you to taste
its nonbeing   hands I give you to mold its breasts and thighs
hearing I give you to hearken to its cries, its desire
body I give you to swallow and digest it, the heart to
love it but the brain to destroy it and to dream
another kind of matter a hypermatter another kind of imagination
the dream to dream itself, a regeneration through dream:

if I were to think the universe blind, this universe would spin
its white globes, its blind planets, in vain, if I were to
think the universe a magnolia, this universe would bloom pink and sweet,
a huge inflorescence in a pearled cup, if I were to think the universe
a game of gravity and spheres, a child would play happily
with balls, cubes and prisms throughout the boundlessness of space,
if I were to wish this universe a Beatrice, a vast and beautiful
woman would drive the masculine worlds mad, if I were to
shout out that the universe is no more than a phantasm, a guffaw of pleasure
and terror would slash through my eardrums: the universe is a medusa
                    swimming,
the universe is a golden clock, it's the dance from under the insteps
of a god, it's a wave,
a vibration
a thought in a bigger thought in a much bigger thought.

Oh, my every organ is crushed, and the world is a metaphysical organ
     in love with its own annihilation,
we tend continuously to transform into light
     into thought to fall back
into repose—death, how brightly you shine!—
but something or somebody from outside and below

still feeds us ceaselessly
    with young matter   with darkness   with chaos.

5.

At the center of the galaxy I discovered the face of a little girl
    a blond Alice with golden curls
laughing raucously   piercingly   much too uproariously
    tumbling through the void   skipping rope in the silent spaces
I heard her joyous peals of laughter   long   lavish
    her desperate shrieks   unremitting
which went on and on and on   which couldn't be stopped
    the reverberating gales of pleasure and terror
of a girl continuously turning into a woman,
    then a fetus, a girl next, and again a woman,
at once with blood-red flowings and ebbings
    at once with vast swaddlings and unfurlings
simultaneously with expulsions and rendings of the tissue
        of the cosmic cocoon.
    For this universe is feminine.

And we are a fetus hearing the mother's weeping
Alice erupting in hilarity   guffawing   laughing to tears
she a fetus too   in a much greater mother.

6.

And all of a sudden, I could no longer see you
I could no longer see your mouth, face, knees, hands
but only a crazed dance, patches of light and shadow
in waves as tremendous ascensions turns and falls
transforming into spume and whirlpools
I saw an oscillating choreography of
waves cresting and breaking golden points fluid lines,
curves prisms bright sparkling ellipses
small dark voids, I saw bottomless abysses
staticky with magnetic buzzing, I felt
heavy dizzying forces, strange high voices,
I saw miniature Milky Ways crossed by soaring colors
galaxies exploding in frantic rainbows,

all these were dancing waving twinkling turning into
you and you were all these,
I was deciphering your brown eyes your pale face your mouth
in that melting gap like a sidereal drawing, like a fata morgana
luminous in the vast darkness   and in that ever-moving dust,
desperate, I stopped to cry out after you, I was no longer alone, you
were there above everything and at last you were happy,
you were roaring like three hilarious nebulae, dancing berserk
in nuclei and lightning flashes, in incandescent particles and
greenish translucent spheres, inside which sacred purple lotuses
flowered in pairs of lovers embracing on their petals,
I was among the luminous spheres
but I was also a corpuscle fallen in love expanded vastly   as that hot loving
space   so as to swallow and contain you   to be one with you
together to give birth   out of a brilliant sphere
a sidereal lotus flower   with another couple embracing on its purple petals
imagining yet another bright sphere   yet another universe.

7.

We set forth   to overtake the sun
    in an invisible spaceship   in an ascending jet
we rose   a vertical path into the blue   the dark
    the void
upwards upwards   higher higher

we saw the earth   an eyeball popped from its socket
    rolling and whistling   an easter egg painted   with
blue stripes   golden sparks   dark shadows
    like a naked encephalon   sadly receding into space

black black   the void the void

we saw the moon   her huge red face   woman's
    a woman fallen in love   her craters, empty seas   her eyes
beseeching   a grieved madonna's   shyly retreating
    into space   then very small and pale

the void the void   infinite infinite

The sun approached, huge   coming close like a prodigious mouth
    of flames   the sun fully upon us   the spaceship incandescent
the sun flowing inside us   our jet caught in a sea
and we melted   evaporated   became sun

the sun was swallowing a sun inside another sun
a golden burning consumption   and we are sun   incandescent darkness
little suns in a bigger sun in a bigger sun
a blinding chasm   sun sun   a blinding chasm   sun sun
wholly sun   sun   altogether sun   sun   absolutely sun

sun   sun   sun   sun   sun

Then everything gets extinguished, in the rapidly cooling darkness
    I hear arising from myself an old voice lamenting
everything is extinction   everything death   everything the void
    rolling its ever-lingering echo   in its fall through space
in the invisible craft   the descending jet   suddenly turning dark
    I hear arising from deep within a childish voice   like a vertical liftoff
everything is life   everything resurrection

sun   over dead souls   only death
sun   over living souls   only life

sun   incandescent matrix   fiery vulva
                    drink me in, swallow me once more.

8.

Then you alone, I alone   in the whole of the universe   lightning-struck
with waterfalls of cascading roars sighs and smiles
filled with blue fires and auroral eruptions
torn by apocalyptic rainbows and long meteoric rainfalls
then you alone, I alone   traversed by spurting jets of blood and obsessions
thunderclaps of thoughts   explosions   rivers of fire
you'll have your space grave.

when the planets turn soft and tremulous
ever-shifting holograms   through which you can observe your trembling hand
and suns steam in transparent strands   gentle rarefied presences
will cool your forehead   the void will flow molten
elastic aromatic and fiery   like the skin of
a pubescent girl   darkness will shine brightly
like blindness suddenly seeing the light of your thought
omnidirectional and overwhelming as in the act of love

then you alone   in such beatitude discovering
your own astonished body, made whole   with blue and red rivers of
corpuscles   plasma   lightning bolts of tendons and nerves
your body, whole   in the fission and fusion of planets
and cells   within intra-atomic tides   and the musics of space
your body, whole   utterly other   otherwise utterly the same
but much vaster   much, much brighter

then I alone   in that cosmic grave   transfigured
into thought   into light   under the light of the Thought
waiting for you   waiting   you will see   other worlds of thought
embracing you   omnidirectional and overwhelming
as in the act of love   or you will see nothing
you'll be free to say Yes   to say No   to be free.

9.

One hour later, gravity finds me again.

I am sitting on the sea wall   at a table buried in drifted sand
     and munching on words   dead dried mollusks   a universe of
dried words   destroyed   by their proximity to the void
     to its cold absolute
all around a red, sonorous sea   words words words   slowly rising
     over the sand   over the ankles
there are dead fish in the water   archaic shells   rusty coins
there are solitary, stray images   flying colors   there are liquid
     graves   in the black and red water   slicks of oil and blood
          scattering the oblique light of the setting sun   into distorting mirrors
the water is rising   I, I am seated at an empty table   waiting   waiting
     for what ?   my mouth fills with blood   the sea rises higher higher
               but
what is the I? the huge wave asks   tumbling purple-red
     over the beaches   nobody nobody   a vast tired voice
replies   like a rustle of leaves   a long
     sidereal yawn   I look all around   nobody's here   only
     a black bird burning its feathers in the distance
everything   everything   a little child whispers   plump and white
     suddenly appeared in a nacreous shell   borne on the waves.

III. And the World

Loved Nevertheless

At sixteen   still part of eternity   standing in tears
on a concrete bridge   across a nearly dry creek bed
a trickle too listless
too shallow   for my measureless grief
my grief at the eternal missed meeting between lover
and beloved   between what mirrors and what gets mirrored
    leaning over the side of the narrow concrete bridge   staring
    staring intensely at the water   the creek's languid trickle
    at the water   staring at the depthless water

On the bottom I could see delicate gray gravel   rusty coins   fine silt
bottles and cans   and an immense pity
for these discarded things   came over me
a vast and terrible pity   as if I were like them
the ugly, long-forgotten things   then immediately
I became them   the trash   stones   coins   bottles and cans
I became one with the bridge   the parched creek
one with the scarlet sunset   the grass withered on the banks
I became pity itself   its innermost essence
or how else should I describe it?
its strange electric vibration   silent waveform shimmering in silent air
    spreading outward   ingathering   dissolving again
    rustling   flowing   murmuring   fading in scarlet.

The empty tin can thrown away in the water   was thrown in me
my own grief submerged deep inside my being
and in the stones   in the twilight sky   in the creek
my single separate sorrow no longer made sense   I myself was the whole
          world
and like lightning   a limitless clarity   electrified my being.
    Then I knew in its stroke   I was loved   loved nevertheless
    loved   by a much vaster love.

In the fullness of the living silence   like a gigantic creature   I asked
    the stones   creek   coins   bridge,
Do you see me   do you want me   do you love me?
In the fullness of the living silence   like a gigantic invisible breath
    the stones   creek   coins   bridge   whispered in my ear,
Do you see us   do you want us   do you love us?

Night Garden

Passing through the forgotten cemetery   through the deserted city   into
        the garden
     among marble gravestones   in the warm darkness
you would not believe me   you doubted my words
     oh, my blossomed hell   lost among T-squares and books
in the vast summer night   wanting to lose me   on the pathways
     behind the hedges   and I, following you like a shadow   wrapped
only in my constant sorrow   among flowers and dark foliage
     in such cloying fragrance   then suddenly you asked me:
how does the wisteria speak? and the honeysuckle? the jasmine?

blue-gray drops shimmered on green darkening leaves
     shadowy faces   the rustle of eyes   curled twisted tongues
undulating   whispering confused night words   we were
soiled with alien words   we were falling
     falling out of love   oh love   stained bed of this world
along the paths   among hedges and heavy perfumes   in darkness

how does the hollyhock sing? what does the cornflower say? and the lily?
     their little striped mouths   white   pink   blue   showing a
        glint of teeth
       their moist, tender depths   sighing   giggling
indifferent in the dark fabric of fragrance   I was translating them for you
     whispering   crying loudly   in multicolor consonants
in sugary aromatic spherical vowels   murmuring   undulating   rising above
     love which is never perfectly round   fragrance which forgets forever
      which blooms light in the flash of an instant
      then fast fades away.

Still, you would not believe me: but the tulip, how does it croon and coo?
        how does
    the lilac chuckle, warble? what does the rose keep whispering?
I was so near you   in the warm darkness   yet far from your body

chirping you   cooing you   warbling you   chanting you   waiting
to be touched gently by a raised green stem   kissed by pollen and
         stamens
     how does Anna burst into flower? as what shade of petals does
         Magdalena open? Maria?
     how does Martha turn into light? Christina? who gathers their
         fragrance?

That I may begin to sing   to intone a new vegetal euphony of goodness
retrieve for you the flowers' ancient green language
     in which you once made me blossom—
         who could ever utter such luminous sweetness?
When we were tulips and lilacs and lilies
     and together we flowered as one in the garden
you were the rough stem   I, your purple calyx
you were the bloom of fluorescence   I, the glistening inflorescence
     opening out in gold   red   blue vibrations   pure sounds   pure scents

simultaneously we would talk together with the scarlet peony of the Earth
     with the sweet narcissus drifts of the stars   with the luxurious orchid
         `   of galaxies
oh love, you who move the immovable   and make the void bloom.

On the pathways darkness   in darkness   among hedges
you had forgotten   and you refused to believe me
     you kept asking me   what is the magnolia starting to sing? the daisies?
         the verbena?
what is going on in their corollas?   steep upward climbs, struggles, deep
         descents
     cries of ecstasy and screams of hate   sometimes prayers and hymns
but from the outside—   only the brilliant color   the consummate form
     a gratuitous gift   flowered for everyone   and for no one   an offering
which a vast hand of air   or a hand of flesh and blood and bone
     could so easily crush between two fingers   could absentmindedly
         pluck the petals from.

On the labyrinthine pathways,   inside the warm darkness   as in a celestial
        cavern
    I was guiding you through the garden,   wrapped only in my all-
        pervading sorrow
when out of the foliage   thousands of voices floated upward to us
    perfumed voices   blue   red   gold voices
    tender voices inviting   imploring   urging gently and insistently
that once more   naked and cleansed   we ascend toward love
love—fiery bridge over blossomed hell
    that I be the moist, newly spaded earth
        where you plant seed and seedling
    that you be the rough green stem and the strong light
        descending far into the warm darkness
    that I be the crown   the calyx   the red-purple corolla
        sparkling in the incandescence of the union
    that we again blossom as the unique inflorescence
        out of which each bud would sprout   each stem   each flower.

Blessed is the land that your hand has dug
    purified earth   refined   exalted
        out of which   together   we would rise
            beyond the world   beyond the deserted city   to the garden of
            light.

The Green Kiosk in the Public Gardens

If this world   is wavelength   arbitrary   the dream
      of a crazed pulsation   an oscillation inside nuclei   intervals and gaps
      like a blind pendulum   swinging between planets of clay
and galactic nightmares   wave following wave
like an ultrasonic frequency enfolding into itself   rustling overtones
      the music of drowned worlds   submerged big-bangs
like sick thought   in the cosmic ocean of thoughts

if this world   of energy   harmony   waves
      like the fleck of spindrift   spread by the flick of an open hand
equivocal   sly   insolent   a joyful swarm of subatomic particles
      turning ironically into each other   playfully dispersing themselves
            through time without end
random   absentminded   indeterminate   like the discharge into the void
      of an entropic memory   dream-laden   supersensitive   utopian
if this world still scorns our crude elementary senses
      striving implausibly to bind together   what this strange universe tears
            apart
desperately   stubbornly   choosing between the great void
      and the infinitesimal void   only that narrow fissure in which
            exhausted   we might sleep   or scream
always reducing   pulsations   wavelengths   antimatter
      to the narrowest bandwidth   an attenuated thread   fragrant   warm
      where we might love   maybe dream

always I will choose this   perception   barbaric and bitter
      stubborn   blind   archaic
so that my eye might glimpse
      in the ocean of vibrations   energies   frequencies
            the teacup from which   melancholy and careworn
                  he has just now taken a sip   a burned-out cigarette
                        hanging carelessly between his lips
                              in the green wooden kiosk   in summer
                                    in the public gardens.

Hyacintha

Her name was Hyacintha, *Iacinta,*
    name of the spicy flower of spring   unfortunate melancholy ephebe
        disseminating his unripe blood throughout the countryside
    and name of a Christian martyr
her name was *Iacinta,* how strange, hyacinth, I was exalted
    as if from a deep breath of perfumed chloroform
her name was Hyacintha   but she ignored everything
cared for nothing.

She lay in the white hospital bed,
she had had four children, didn't know anything about sex, genitals,
cycles, pills, all those mysterious things,
she was sallow and thin, had straw-colored hair,
almost a peasant, was afraid of the lancet and of blood,
desired to have no more children. I asked her,
do you know how it feels to be a hyacinth?
Hyacintha looked at me, startled.

She lay in the white hospital bed
    terrorized by her own body   ashamed.

Just because her name was Hyacintha, *Iacinta,*
    spicy flower of spring plucked from snow-covered fields,
        handsome ill-fated ephebe,
        immaculate Christian martyr,
I taught her about genitals, cycles and pills,
in the bed full of hyacinth petals
I helped her
        to disseminate
            her blood.

Dark Orchid

Why, every time I see him approaching me in the street
    or maybe when I think I've spotted his back in the crowd,
       among shoulders and auto tires, asphalt and shop windows—
why does a terrible dread overwhelm me   a strange inner heat, a wave of
           nausea,
    and all at once, against my own volition,   I cross to the other side of
       the street?

The spheres of my eyes darken; my pupils narrow and throb;
    a cold tunnel inside me opens into a funnel toward chaos.
As if the nearness of his face, so long desired,
      would mean destruction, the end.
Who inside me is afraid of you?
Exactly what does this somebody fear?
And why, alongside this fear, such great desire for you?

My pupils narrow;   icy chaos absorbs me;   a void;
    then a hot vortex melts my will   and my flesh;
      suddenly, against my own desire,   I cross the street.
As if the nearness of his body, so long dreamed of,
    would be like an electron's instantaneous collapse into the nucleus,
      or the accelerating plunge   of a too massive planet   into its sun,
        absorbed by the unplumbed darkness   of an extinguished eye.
Of what kind of antimatter is your gaze composed?
What electrical charge   opposite to mine   do your beautiful hands hold?
What intense negative field   makes the negation I am   so sharply feel
       its attraction?

As if, touching you, I would arrive at the ultimate stage of my evolution.
As if, in fusing us, the universe would suddenly screech to a halt
    and lurch aside from its steady disfigurement: in a flash
    its old, blowsy, drooping orchid would be reabsorbed into a point:
      that point, vanishing, would die happy.

My eyes, my thinking spheres, grow dim; luminous chaos
    absorbs me; a void;   still I cross the street.
Who inside me wishes to be destroyed through you?
Who desires to be unified with itself?
    And to burst out of us into space, a solar flare?

Dark, destructive cosmic orchid   disintegration which is reintegration
    fusion which is confusion   annihilation of which I am terrified
        even while desiring it so much:
the sole means that   killing me   would give me new life.

Is it only through death I can touch your love?

Couple Poem

1.

The old woman is telling the much younger woman
about her past: tender red lips and
hot foamy rapids
    which now she can look upon only while weeping.
In the ill-furnished room   time slows down   slows down
    turns back; stops short for a suspended instant
    and suddenly reveals a ghastly countenance.
At that moment the young woman sees
        the huge translucent Vein
    through which she and the old woman and
    the impoverished room and the meager, sordid things around them
        together with the entire city and rivulets
like colorless blood   incomprehensible   a monotonous murmuring
    flow out of a small, obscure mouth
            into a dark, bottomless mouth.

2.

The old woman is telling the much younger woman
about her past: savage diseases and cruel operations
chilling complaints about medicines and death.
In the austere room the young woman absentmindedly
    listens to her:
        she is thinking of love   love   and all at once
        she would love everything around her   the chairs, the table
    the old woman and her decrepit, wretched things
        the grimy window   the city.
And suddenly she imagines death
        with strange, unbridled joy; a constriction
        at her overawed heart   a fierce fiery wave floods her body
      as in puberty   when in a secret fever she daydreamed

of her first man   her first love-making.
At that very moment the young woman sees
        dazzling Blood   incomprehensible   foamy
        flow out of a small, obscure mouth
            into a vast, illuminated mouth.

An Amphitheater in Greece

An amphitheater in Greece   where I try to forget my suffering
     hiding myself behind myrtle trees and slabs of white stone
among the torrent of tourists   Asian   Nordic   oh, my love
     my lost Delos   this echo of voices   concentric   sonorous
I was gazing at the empty stage of the arena   dark and gold   if you, you

are like me   and I am your perfect reflection   why,
     why all these imperfect copies?   the repeated out-of-focus photographs
     of our glittering shroud   imbued
with the red burn mark of our mouths   perfect infinity signs
     why this myriad   of fragmentary distorting mirrors?
Blind splinters   on which   you still seek the image of your face.

An amphitheater in Greece   oh, suffering   from the highest stone step
     the world opened like a bible   of blue rivers and mountains
a bible of women and men   in a torrent   Asian   Nordic
     flowing from the four points of the compass   the echo   concentric
          sonorous   in the empty center of the arena   the golden void
precious vomit   of your mouth   red and unpitying
     where curses and prayers are one   are nothing   why?
If I am your perfect mirror   then this blind cosmos
     this mirror among mirrors   millions and millions   is itself
your unfaithfulness.   And the sin is yours.

That you whisper to me,   be! be!   and I burst forth with you
     that you whisper to it,   be! be!   and the world truly exists
despite my desire   flowing from the four points of the compass
that I whisper to it,   no   be no more! be no more!
     but the world goes on   this Delos of darkness and gold

only by the mischance   the deficiency   the failure of your love.

Ana Ipătescu of the Block

for the Romanian women poets of my generation

In shalwar,
on cheap jute carpets, among stained napkins, crusts
    of bread and empty glasses,
half asleep, your voice a whisper,
    small and wistful as if fit for the soft brain
    of a man, a little silken bell tied
    to the burly neck of the beast, you preached
petty chamber revolutions, bodily rebellions, imaginary insurrections
and other tender phantoms, while those around you stumbled
    on the carpets, fell, got up again with comically measured paces,
    opened another bottle of vodka there in the dark
of your bare apartment in the blocks at the wild outskirts of the city, books
    and newspapers strewn across the floor, where no one except your mother
    dared straighten up, between two apparitions,
two fights with painters, poets, beggars, strutting young sultans,

Ana Ipătescu of the block, 1848 revolutionary, odalisque
    with the black green blue sad eyes of a mummy
painted moments ago, heretical icon, *femme fatale*
    with small breasts, too small for the big world,
with your charm, glamour, artifices squandered in cafés,
    sighs, baby talk, writing about mothers, sisters, serving girls
    and young ladies, about the waterline and
    the final armor of being, the Other, salvaged verbs, hypermatter
and the tribulations of a poor young student, a mere girl,

you saw yourself already on Parnassus, on gold and purple clouds
among civilizing heroes, melancholy angels and madonnas
on an azure pedestal the focus of silent adoration, a paper child in your arms,
and from all the baby talk and invective, fancied illnesses, trinkets
and velvet, that there should arise a strange odor of blood, sap, sweat,
lullaby and battle song, funeral march, cologne and moral law—

teacher, unemployed, museum curator, engineer, nurse,
again a teacher, between two commutes, two buses,
two railroad stations, platforms, trains,
withdrawn from the world but no less magnetic, dressed or undressed,
vicious yet child-like, like a double-edged truth,
like the descent of the spirit into the Virgin, with your small voice,
your sensual mouth of a mummy painted moments ago—

modern vestal of the word, mother of the wounded,
sophia to a cadre of poets, slovenly yet fatal,
Ana Ipătescu of the block, 1848 revolutionary, odalisque,

Helen without Troy, Tristan without Isolde, Mary without Providence.

That you should trouble our sleep, our unconscious, our weekends,
    with your crackpot laws, discovered in sanatoriums in the mountains,
about ultra-matter and the disintegration of decayed cultures into swarms,
        about the killer verb and the evil that does not, no, does not exist,
freedom alone exists and a deafening silence and the acceleration
    through poetry of the end of the world.

Prophetess of the boudoir, scarecrow with maternal whims,
protecting unborn poets and martyrs in a commonwealth
of nations in your bare apartment on the top floor
somewhere at the outskirts of the city where hope runs dry,
slovenly and scatterbrained, elite model, fatuous pyre,
glossy cover of a pagan magazine,
crumpled sheets of paper covered by minuscule handwriting
launched like fabulous torpedoes into the mouth of the leviathan
that quivers with pleasure and giggles, caressing you:
wise and silly hummingbird, little silken bell
        tied to the neck of the beast:

how red your lips, how sparkling your eyes,
how vast and kind you are as you sit on the red-hot iron chair
magnanimously officiating at chamber revolutions on the ultimate floor of

heaven,
among painters poets unborn orphans swaggering young sultans
at the outskirts of the world, receiving exuberant crowds with your veins
              sliced and spread wide,
that their enticing warmth should suddenly dislodge the paving stones
of the piazzas, those places that forget, forget all too quickly,
should stain bright red the walls of cities and the pristine brilliance of springs
flowing into oceans, an enigma, a tender drop
of insidious blood,

Ana Ipătescu of the block, 1848 revolutionary, odalisque.

Psalm

Again in the glory of morning, on the Avenue of Victory

stepping into the leavening of the crowd, the warm ocean
of living solitude, its wild, living waters,
this time without portent, without purple and flowers,
there comes upon me a towering shame, heavy and faceless,
an all-pervading, unbearable shame—
like a scarecrow in a field, cloud-tall and thin,
like a sudden terror, the ice of mercury in my veins,
he comes and looks me in the eye with a huge, chilling gaze,
he looks at me from high above and covers me with an ocean of eyes and
                sea foam,
as if in the shrill of sirens, the hiss and rumble of cars, in the glory
of academies and office towers, the world would reveal itself
as a colossal mound of shame.

Oh, trivial individual fear, fetid swamp, dark grave of rotting garbage,
all-pervading fear of people, ocean of mud drowning history and utopias,
precious moment of my misery now,
last judgment of my belated awakening.

That I should kneel on the Avenue of Victory, on the wet sidewalk,
here among all of you on the cold asphalt, to beg forgiveness,
there must be a reason for my guilt, I have to have made some mistake,
something immense and forgotten, something old, fraught with horror,
that I ask you for forgiveness, I, a single tiny cell among all of you
who are the cells in me, you who are my church,
a cathedral dome rustling with a myriad of whispering cells,
a mighty dome in human form.

That I should pray, in this universe devoid of prayer,
where I have no one to pray to; who, then, can forgive me?
What is the name of this boundless, unpardonable guilt?

That I should ask pardon of the crowd: if you refuse me, who will assume
this unendurable shame, the tall, thin scarecrow, and burn it within?
If you don't forgive me, then something bigger than you,
somebody much much bigger, will absolve me,
a man cresting like a wave, the rustle of a myriad of whispering cells,
an enormous, transparent man, the perfect form of the world.

That I should kneel on the Avenue of Victory; that I should learn how to pray,
to beg for absolution; that towering shame, heavy and faceless, the scarecrow.
But I cannot kneel in the street, here on the wet sidewalk,
no, something keeps preventing me: something dead and putrefied.
Oh, trivial individual fear, your fetid swamp, grave of feelings and guilt,
all-pervading fear of people, your chaotic, unconscious self-pity,
your long, unbroken slumber, our reluctant, phlegmatic awakening,
your chaotic, unconscious love, the lukewarm sea foam swept away
by fear, guilt, shame, something keeps me from prayer.

One day, in the glory of morning, on some Avenue of Victory
purified by the fire of the crowd, its painful ocean of hot intensity,
kneeling easily on the cold, wet asphalt,
without dirtying myself, feeling no guilt, no pain,
as in a luminous cathedral of glass,
below a lofty, translucent dome,
something much bigger than you and than I
            will forgive and be forgiven.
Something like a sky-tall, invisible man,
the melancholic cresting wave of a myriad of whispering cells,
            something like divine, cosmic love.

Or maybe, long ago, I have already fallen here to my knees?

By Hope

Between a sacred lake of blue   and the ghastly squirming
in a tanning vat   all the love in the world
is comprised: all your love.
I can admit both within me   straw and crystal
silt and gold   excrement and sun,
for diamond is awakened coal.

It's spring   I wander the streets   myself blossomed   I mingle
with the swirling green crowd   everything looks beautiful to me   the sun
speckles your faces with flashing mirrors   intersections sparkle
in a cascade of sunrays   shop windows reflect fireworks   coruscations
exploding in all directions   as overwhelming   as love
the streets form lazy rivers of molten crystal   frantic rainbows jet
from trees   lawns diffuse the dust of crushed emerald
into the air   tulips in flower beds shimmer like fiery rubies
I'm on the point of crying out   buildings appear living whirlpools
of bright multicolor sparks   cars turn into pinwheels of gold flecks
the asphalt shines with jasper, opal, agate   walls disclose layer upon layer
of jewels and precious stones   I'm on the point of crying out: look,
someone must be rolling pearls on the sidewalks   under our soles and heels
someone must be powdering peoples' faces with glitter
someone must be igniting the city to incandescence   everything
has become translucent   everything looks unbearably beautiful to me
this beauty an immense gift   free
offered in all directions   as overwhelming   as love.

I wander the streets   mingle with the radiant crowd
it's spring   men and women alike   are smoky crystals
gliding down the alleys   flickering between chiaroscuro and light
they promenade   with soft puffy diamonds   in their strollers
couples seem to me an obscure miracle
this miracle walks multiplied through stores and outdoor markets
liquid gold pours out of pockets and purses

I caress you tenderly in my mind   that you really exist
astonishes me   all these couples are us
ourselves replicated as in a never-ending stream
a current of molten crystal that spreads in long rivulets
flowing through city district and field
the two of us endlessly mirrored   a glistening magma
a river of awakening light   flooding outwards into the universe
in all directions   as overwhelming   as love.
The sun stains our faces with dazzling halos   it's spring
I'm on the point of crying out:

If the world is a river of fluidity   parallel mirrors
a long immersion   between the sacred lake of blue and the black tanning vat,
and if time is *aqua fortis*   the royal bath   in which
our bodies are plunged   waiting for their slow transparency,
yes, if we are but extinguished rubies   opaque emeralds
waiting for the corrosive acid   for the cosmic laser
to carve facets in us   to polish us till we gleam
or raw unexposed film   sleeping negatives
on which the flashgun of the void   must fix its brilliance,
and if in the end a blinding maternal light in turn waits for us
pure light   permanent ecstasy   an hallucinatory awakening
in all directions   as overwhelming   as love,
it's spring   the sun speckles faces with sequins and glints
I wander the streets blinded   I mingle with the radiant crowd:

with my enormous insane hope   my absurd indestructible hope
like an ancestral water   corrosive   intoxicating every cell of my being
I add myself to your small weak hope   drowned in ancient terrors
your unbelieving hope   easily shattered   like a thin sheet of ice
melting before the least premonition of fear
that we consummate this life   this universe   not by dominion of this world
nor by darkness   nor death   but by hope.

For diamond is awakened coal.

Chaosmos

In the end
      disorder reaches perfection
languages dissolve into the music   of wind
      chaos attains pure splendor.

In the end   out of the whirlwinds   whirlpools   evolution
      the world screeches to a halt   a fixed image
waters   the heavens   cities   hang suspended
      the entire universe consummates
                  in a
      daring and profound photograph.

He holds up the print   still wet
      examines it for a long, long time
         examines himself for as long a time
         and gulps it down.

IV. Post-Manifesto

A Vast Reader

A reader will read me one day,
but not a *semblable*, a brother lost among upper-case type, diagonals, hyphens,
diaereses and similar marks, a hypocrite reader overwhelmed by phonemes and
paradigms, seeking nostalgically, desperately, for colored vowels and old-fash-
ioned perfect rhymes

his eye hypnotized by sonorous images, as if by his own baby picture, pink,
plump and naked on a blanket embellished with flowers, his mother's pride, a
fading snapshot in which he would also like to behold his gold braid, his titles,
his medals, his properties and the entire ripe splendor of his ripe maturity

rummaging for oxymorons and synecdoches, but above all for metonymies, the
most modish of tropes, those precious ridiculous ladies, the crook of his
index finger between the lines as if digging raisins and honeyed poppyseed out
of a Christmas cake, as eager as an amateur astronomer ogling the heavens
through his small telescope trying to pinpoint his personal star in the night's
milky galactic ocean

and then measuring, with a symbolist, psychoanalytic, poststructuralist,
deconstructionist lens and some flimsy strips of litmus paper, the spectrum
of radio waves, infrared, ultraviolet and ineffable, of an enormous mountain
of printed pages, his sacred wastepaper, his harmless, aseptic drug, soothing
and mellow, satiating the millions of his brain cells and bibliophilic emotion-
al labyrinths

establishing the eternity of words by means of the geometric regularity of
grains of sand, the structure of crystals, because of the color of pollen and
the electromagnetic fields forever captured in the clay of prehistoric pottery,
thanks to carbon 14 and the number and thickness of the rings in tree trunks,
by dint of the petrified fragments of skeletons and the richness of phosphates
in dejecta, all these readily becoming fluorescent under the black light of
Wood's lamp.

A reader will read us one day,
not a *semblable*, a brother, but one far more vast, more enormous, from much
farther away, leafing through the pages of our lives as through miscellaneous
yellowed newspapers, discarded pages covered with tiny holographic lines that
the wind scatters every which way, stringing us in sentences and phrases, in
peoples and histories comprehensible only to him, like a necklace of true
pearls and faux pearls adorning the scrawny throat of eternity, deciphering
patiently and precisely, like a laser, all texts, books, chronicles, births, deaths
and resurrections, one who will taste their small drop of honey, clear or cloud-
ed, bitter or sweet, on his harsh, impossible tongue

in a deafening silence, like terrestrial hurricanes swallowing deserts and
idioms, jungles and metropolises, cosmic tornadoes extinguishing luxuriant
nebulae, galaxies in flower, a withered, apocalyptic whisper like the bone-dry
exhalation in the nostrils of the last man as he contemplates the world's para-
ble and dereliction, yet also like the moist gasp in the mouth of the first new
man inhaling, voraciously, the rebirth of the sky, the auroral arch of the earth,
the first resurrected vowel

he will encompass in the boundless blue crystal of his eye, and also the single
strand of hair that the abandoned woman, in her piety, picks with tweezers
from the scarf her lover left behind, the hyperbolic mind of the species, the
sophisticated chess of civilizations, the poetical systems of nature, Morel's
invention, desperate utopias and fairy-tale nightmares—every one of these
things he will encompass in the dazzling crystalline lens of his single, all-
embracing eye—and the mustard seed, too, the dot on the letter *i* and this
planet

weighing their suffering and their love, more than anything else their love, and
their foolishness in daring to die in order to live, to live again in something
much too unbelievable, abstruse, illiterate; then, when only metaphor still can
bear the crushing weight of past time, its endless gaze far behind, its endless
gaze far ahead, when only poetry will go on pulsing through its veins the
blood of resurrection:

I shall wait for that reader.

Notes on the Poems

Portrait of a Flash, pp. 44–45

Chitila and Grivița are suburbs of Bucharest.

The Avenue of Victory (Calea Victoriei)—also referred to in the poem "Psalm" near the end of the third section of this book (pp. 82–83)—is the main and most fashionable street of Bucharest, running north-south through the center of the city.

In Brâncovean Style, pp. 46–47

Constantine Brâncoveanu, Prince of Wallachia from 1688-1714, was a skilled diplomat who fostered education and culture; he is known for the Brâncovean architectural style that is an ornate synthesis of Western and Oriental styles, combining Renaissance and Baroque elements along with traditional Romanian forms.

Ana Ipătescu of the Block, pp. 79–81

Ana Ipătescu was a famous woman combatant of the 1848 revolution in Romania, who led a rebellion that made an assault on the Dealul Spirii ("Spirea Hill") in Bucharest, where the events of 1848 began in Romania. It is now the location of the Parliament building, originally built as the communist dictator Nicolae Ceaușescu's "House of the People," an incredibly huge edifice that matched his megalomania.

A Vast Reader, pp. 89–90

The French *semblable*—literally "fellow man," according to a French-English dictionary—connotes so much because of Baudelaire's famous provocative line in *Les Fleurs du Mal* (*"Hypocrite lecteur,—mon semblable,—mon frère!"*), a triple epithet perhaps also recognizable to English readers from Eliot's *The Waste Land*. Cârneci's Romanian original uses the French word, and thus it has been carried over in our English. English versions of Baudelaire's poem often render *semblable* as "double," "twin," or "likeness," sandwiched between "hypocrite reader" and "my brother."

Wood's lamp is a device that emits long-wave ultraviolet radiation, commonly called black light.

Morel's invention is the holographic device that makes a subject eternal by destroying it, in the novel of that title by the Argentinean author, Adolfo Bioy Casares.

The Author

Magda Cârneci, born in 1955, is a widely acclaimed Romanian poet, as well as a prominent essayist and art historian and critic. Cârneci has become the leading poet among the gifted group of writers who began their careers in Romania's bleak 1980s, communism's final decade. Her first two books of poetry, *Hypermateria* (1980) and *A Deafening Silence* (1985), met with much praise for their originality and visionary imagination, as did *Chaosmos* (1992, reprinted in 2004), viewed as soaring, volcanic, authentic. After serving as a visiting professor of modern Romanian literature in Paris, in 2006 she became deputy director of the Romanian Cultural Institute there. She has been awarded grants from the Fulbright Foundation, Getty Trust, Soros Foundation, European Union, French government and Cité Internationale des Arts in Paris. She has also authored monographs on art and curated major exhibitions in Europe. Cârneci's poems have been translated into thirteen languages and included in numerous anthologies. This is the first book-length publication of Cârneci's work in the English-speaking world.

The Translator

Adam J. Sorkin has translated more than twenty-five books of contemporary Romanian literature. He has won the Corneliu M. Popescu Translation Prize of The Poetry Society, London, as well as the Kenneth Rexroth Memorial Translation Prize and honors in Romania and Moldova. Two of his books were shortlisted for the Weidenfeld Prize, Oxford. Sorkin's work has been supported by the Academy of American Poets, the Rockefeller and Witter Bynner Foundations, the Arts Council of England and the Fulbright Program. The National Endowment for the Arts awarded him a fellowship for *Chaosmos*. The *Times Literary Supplement* has termed Sorkin "the most sensitive current translator of Romanian poetry into English," and Romanian poet/novelist Mircea Cărtărescu has written, "he is the best translator of poetry from Romanian into English . . . . His translations are unique in their fine balance between accuracy and poetic beauty." Sorkin is Distinguished Professor of English at Penn State Delaware County.